The Messenger

The Messenger

DAPHANNY C. BAKER

J MERRILL

J Merrill Publishing, Inc.
434 Hillpine Drive
Columbus, OH 43207
www.JMerrill.pub

Library of Congress Control Number: 2024902168
ISBN-13: 978-1-961475-15-1 (Paperback)
ISBN-13: 978-1-961475-16-8 (eBook)

Book Title: The Messenger
Author: Daphanny C. Baker

Dedication

*The dedication of this book is threefold, there are three very
significant people to whom I credit in inspiring me to pursue
these writings.*

Tyrone t. Steals

*You brought the word from the Lord to me during one church
anniversary service: I am to write at least three Books, Saith the
Lord. My teacher told me when I was little that I should become
a writer; It never struck a chord, but when you allowed God to
validate this message, my spirit immediately agreed.*

Brandi Prichett

*You gave me the freedom to speak candidly with you—words
from Heaven—many, many moons ago. I am grateful that you
trusted me with the matters of your heart and allowed me to
provide you with the guidance and divine insight...You allowed
me to be a messenger.*

Betty J. Lee (Mamas)

Thank you so much for accepting the assignment to help me with the birthing of my ministry. Your words to me are always, "God knows" and "Keep going." You have always provided me with the guidance I need to fulfill my calling as God's Messenger.

Contents

Foreword

There was a spirit of greatness in First Lady Baker
that I could tell the moment I met her. For her, it matters
who she is. There is a similar thread running across her
personality, work ethic, leadership in the workplace and in
her ministry, and her roles as a wife, mother, and friend
— "excellence." Excellence is the fabric of who she is. Because
she is a woman of excellence, she is faithful! She has a
Godly Character! She has integrity! She sees it through and
stands in faithfulness in the most difficult trials! She is a
good steward of every opportunity that the Lord sends into
her life! She is one of the strongest women I know. She will
not waiver in adversity, she will not bow down to Satan
because she is not weak. She is a friend that sticks closer
than a brother. This book has been published because of her
faithfulness, her integrity, and above all her excellence in
her obedience to Christ. She has been through some things
and has not tapped out! She has chosen to let the Lord use
her as a vessel. As Paul said, "follow me as I follow Christ."
First Lady Baker's life is such that others are following her
as she follows Christ! First Lady Baker is saying, let me

show you what that looks like! This book will be a blessing to countless people, and it is an honor to share these words in this foreword.

Do not stop with simply reading this book, but we are blessed to be a blessing! Share it with others!

Janet Lynn Cordell-Bryan
December 2023

Are You Stretchable?

I Peter 1:6–9 Living Bible: *"So be truly glad! There is wonderful joy ahead, even though the going is rough for a while down here. These trials are only to test your faith, to see whether or not it is strong and pure. It is being tested as fire tests gold and purifies it—and your faith is far more precious to God than mere gold; so, if your faith remains strong after being tried in the test tube of fiery trials, it will bring you much praise and glory and honor on the day of His return. You love Him even though you have never seen Him; though not seeing Him, you trust Him; and even now you are happy with the inexpressible joy that comes from heaven itself. And your further reward for trusting Him will be the salvation of your souls."*

When I was a kid, I would watch "The Incredible Hulk." Whenever uncomfortable, he would turn green, grow, and stretch out of his clothes, becoming unrecognizable and incredibly strong.

God is trying to bring you to a place where you become so uncomfortable where you are that you will grow and become unrecognizable! He wants you to have such strength that you can and will resist the wiles of the enemy. You'll be strong enough to cast your cares upon God, and you won't just accept any old diagnosis, but you'll be able to say, "By His stripes, I am healed."

Job 1:8 says, *"And the Lord said to Satan, 'Have you considered my servant Job, that there is none like him on the earth, a blameless and upright man, who fears God and turns away from evil?"*

So many times, we blame the enemy for what we're going through when God may have orchestrated your stretching! And as you can see here, Job was a good man and minding his business.

Often, people may ask, "What did I do? What sin did I commit?" But in fact, God is stretching your faith and showing you that if you are obedient, He will bless you far greater than the trial. Just imagine if Job had cursed God and died as people advised him to; he would've never received the extreme blessing at the end of it all. People can get into your business and make you miss out on your reward. Keep your eye on the prize and follow the leading of the Lord.

What is the definition of stretch? To cause to extend from one place to another or across a given space; to extend over a given time.

When you stretch something, a degree of elasticity must be involved, or it will break. What is elasticity? Flexibility; adaptability.

So, before God even decided to stretch you, He knew how much you could take. He knew you were flexible enough and would adapt to what He was trying to do in your life. He trusted you with this, and He knew you would not break or break in this storm! If He allowed it (which He did), then you've got this. What makes you unique and set apart is that He (God) considered you; since He did, He's equipped you for it. He will not be an embarrassment to Himself, so He sent the best one for the job — "YOU!"

He said He would not put any more on us than we can bear, so if He's stretching you, you will come out on top. Let God perfect and establish you!

1 Peter 5:10: *"And the God of all grace, who called you to His eternal glory in Christ, after you have suffered a little while, will Himself restore you and make you strong, firm, and steadfast."*

After you've suffered a little while... I know His 'little while' may seem like a long time, and you're wondering when this trial will be over, but what lesson will you learn if He stops it right in the middle? There's a blessing in the press! There's a reason for your season! There's double for your trouble! You are victorious in every sense of the word!

You'll never know how strong you are until you've been tested. You can't share your testimony unless you've been tested! Until you go through the pain, what can you tell me about the promise? If you've never been sick, how would you know He heals?

Romans 8:28 says, *"And we know that all things work together for good to them that love God, to them who are the called according to His purpose."*

So, if you're "the called," all you face is for a purpose. Whether to build character, increase your faith, prepare you for the next level, or bring glory to God's name, there is a blessing in the stretch! So, stretch it out and wait for your reward!

Don't Tap Out

G alatians 6:9 (KJV): *"Be not deceived; God is not mocked: for whatsoever a man soweth, that shall he also reap. For he that soweth to his flesh shall of the flesh reap corruption; but he that soweth to the Spirit shall of the Spirit reap life everlasting. And let us not be weary in well doing: for in due season, we shall reap, if we faint not."*

The New Living Translation version says in verse 9 (my focal point), *"So let's not get tired of doing what is good. At just the right time, we will reap a harvest of blessings if we don't give up."*

I know things may get hard and uncomfortable, and you might feel like calling it quits, but...

- We can't get tired!
- We can't throw in the towel!
- We can't walk away!
- We definitely cannot bow down to the enemy!

If you remain faithful and stay in the race, there is something in it for you. Paul said in Philippians 3:14 (KJV), *"I press toward the mark for the prize of the high calling of God in Christ Jesus."*

So, what does it mean to press? To continue doing something in a determined way. To hurry forward:

- I press... when I'm hurting!
- I press... when things are bad!
- I press... when I don't know what else to do!
- I JUST PRESS!!!

1 Peter 5:8 (KJV) says, *"Be sober, be vigilant; because your adversary the devil, as a roaring lion, walketh about, seeking whom he may devour."*

But get this! The scripture says, "AS" a roaring lion... He's not even a real lion! So why are we scared? Why do we give power over us to something that has no power over us? Why are we afraid of something that's pretending to be something? AS a roaring lion!!!

Satan also pretends to be good to get you to do bad things. 2 Corinthians 11:13-15 (KJV) states, *"For such are false apostles, deceitful workers, transforming themselves into the apostles of Christ. And no marvel; for Satan himself is transformed into an angel of light. Therefore it is no great thing if his ministers also be transformed as the ministers of righteousness..."*

There are so many that are not real for Christ—having a form of godliness but denying the power thereof! Don't let this be you!!

- No anointing!
- No fruit!

- No fuel!
- No power!
- No substance!
- No real worship!

Just walking around, tricking and deceiving people!

Matthew 4:3 (KJV) says, *"And when the tempter came to him, he said, 'If thou be the Son of God, command that these stones be made bread."*

Satan's foolery didn't trick Christ, and neither should we. He tells him to "be gone!!" and we can too!! Resist the devil, and he will flee!! And casting down every imagination!

When this topic, "Don't Tap Out," came to mind, I first thought about Ju-jitsu... Ju-jitsu is the art of weaponless fighting that employs holds, throws, and paralyzing blows to subdue or disable an opponent and aims to influence the opponent to tap out.

Do you know that the enemy studies you, learns your moves, likes and dislikes, and daily routines so he can get you into compromising positions and back you into a wall so you will give up and tap out?

Psalms 144:1 (KJV) says, *"Blessed be the LORD my strength, which teacheth my hands to war, and my fingers to fight."* So, whatever the enemy throws at me, I am equipped for the battle.

Don't tap out!

- Don't give in to him!
- Don't let him trick you!
- Reposition yourself. Take back your control!

Put on Your Armor!

E phesians 6:10-12 (KJV): *"Finally, my brethren, be strong in the Lord, and in the power of his might. Put on the whole armor of God, that ye may be able to stand against the wiles of the devil."*

This verse appeals to believers to withstand Satan's attacks by strengthening their faith and being equipped with God's armor. It serves as a reminder that the spiritual powers of evil in the world are our enemies, not each other.

The whole armor comprises six pieces, symbolically safeguarding us from spiritual attacks.

Here are the six pieces:

- He gave us the Belt of Truth—this was the first piece of the armor because you have nothing without the truth!
- He gave us the Breastplate of Righteousness to protect our hearts, for the issues of life come out of them.

- He gave us the Shoes of the Gospel to protect our feet — "Yea, though I walk through the valley of the shadow of death, I will fear no evil."
- He gave us the Shield of Faith, representing our faithfulness to God. For without it, we cannot please Him.
- He gave us the Helmet of Salvation to protect our minds from the enemy's attacks.
- The last one is the Sword of the Spirit. What would you do without your sword? Your Bible supplies you with everything you need to survive in this world and make it through.

We are equipped for this! We are prepared for this! We're up for anything the enemy throws our way because we are protected in the most critical areas.

This means:

- Any jab!
- Any blow!
- Any stab!
- ANYTHING!

Psalms 18:39 (KJV) says, *"For thou hast girded me with strength unto the battle: thou hast subdued under me those that rose up against me."*

So, this lets us know that whatever comes, I'm armed because HE has armed us!

There are four seasons, and in these four seasons, you dress accordingly as the weather changes.

- Winter: wear a heavy coat, gloves, boots, and a scarf if it gets too cold.
- Spring: you wear a light jacket or sweater and may carry an umbrella if the weather calls for showers.
- Summer: you wear short-sleeved shirts, sunglasses, and sandals and might need sunscreen depending on the heat.
- Fall: you'll have a lovely cardigan for cooler evenings, along with denim and ankle boots.

You're now ready!

The same goes for entering a war zone—you must be prepared and geared up. War zones are hazardous and erratic environments. To keep safe, it's critical to stay alert and ready.

You don't have time to run back and get anything; you've got to stay ready, so you won't have to get ready. An enemy in battle against you will not wait while you say, "Hold on while I run and get my gear!" or "Hold on while I tie my shoe!" This would be a perfect and suitable time for them to launch an "all-out" attack because you were unprepared.

Don't let the enemy catch you unprepared; he's been studying you and knows when you're not ready.

"And David was greatly distressed, for the people spoke of stoning him, because all the people were bitter in soul, each for his sons and daughters. But David strengthened himself in the Lord his God." (1 Samuel 30:6, KJV)

David fortified himself in the Lord, even amidst severe hardship and warfare. Have we forgotten that in these difficult circumstances, we should grab our shields, proclaim the message of Jesus to ourselves, supplant the enemy's lies with the truth, and build ourselves up in the Lord?

Christ gives us power. He treats us wonderfully and compassionately. He is strong when we are weak.

"Not Perfect but Pressing"

Philippians 3:14 (KJV): *"I press toward the mark for the prize of the high calling of God in Christ Jesus."*

This means we are determined to become more like Christ and follow His purpose. We are not perfect, but increasingly pressing to be like Him. God's will for us is to become like Christ. He will work in our lives to make it happen, but we must also put in some effort. God has all authority. His goal for us is to follow in the footsteps of His son, Jesus Christ. This verse is a critical reminder for us to keep our eyes on Christ and to trail Him with all our hearts. It is easy to get unfocused by the things of this world, but we must keep in mind our goal, which is to become more like Christ and fulfill His purpose for us.

Philippians 4:13 (KJV): *"I can do all things through Christ which strengtheneth me."*

This is to remind us we have the strength for all things and that we can continue in any circumstances by depending on Christ, who gives us the strength. Often, we view our situations as being more significant than God. We feel like we have no hope or one to turn to; but in reality, we can turn to God, who will give us strength through any situation.

Jeremiah 32:17 (ESV): *"Ah, Lord GOD! It is you who have made the heavens and the earth by your great power and by your outstretched arm! Nothing is too hard for you."*

Nothing is too hard for God! Think of the most challenging trial you've ever been through; YOU MADE IT THROUGH! You felt like you would never make it out, wondering how you would pay a bill or return from a setback. You're here reading this, so guess what? You made it.

Daniel 3:23-25 (KJV): *"And these three men, Shadrach, Meshach, and Abednego, fell down bound into the midst of the burning fiery furnace. Then Nebuchadnezzar the king was astonished, and rose up in haste, and spake, and said unto his counsellors, 'Did not we cast three men bound into the midst of the fire?' They answered and said unto the king, 'True, O king.' He answered and said, 'Lo, I see four men loose, walking in the midst of the fire, and they have no hurt; and the form of the fourth is like the Son of God."*

The three men trusted God, remained faithful even in the fire, and refused to worship idol gods. We must be determined that no matter how hot it gets, we will stand for righteousness and not waver in our faith. The phrase "Do not waver in faith" is found in the Bible twelve times. The term means to hold fast to one's faith and resist letting ambiguity or worry get in the way. The expression is often employed to uplift people's faith in God and to hold fast to their convictions. It is also used to reassure people that their faith is essential to who they are and that they shouldn't allow adversity to weaken their faith. Many people love the expression, "I'm not perfect!" and they are precisely correct. However, we mustn't stay there; we're not perfect, but we should strive daily to be like Christ, never giving up on being like Him.

To keep from stumbling and falling, a runner in a race should not continuously look back to see what is behind them. Instead, they are looking straight ahead, concentrating on the goal. Philippians 3:13 (KJV) states, *"Brethren, I count not myself to have apprehended: but this one thing I do, forgetting those things which are behind, and reaching forth unto those things which are before."*

This scripture is regularly applied to encourage individuals to let go of their past and focus on what is ahead.

Why do we, as Christians, focus more on what's behind than what's forward? Keeping a spiritual focus is a significant struggle that all Christians face. No one is exempt. It can be very distracting to be in this physical world. The ups and downs frequently lead us on an alternate path than what would benefit us as Christians most. We are sons and daughters of the Most High, and our conduct should reflect that.

Philippians 4:12 (NIV): *"I know what it is to be in need, and I know what it is to have plenty. I have learned the secret of being content in any and every situation, whether well fed or hungry, whether living in plenty or in want."*

In and through all, we must trust God! Things will not always look like we want them to or go how we want them to. Still, the Bible says in 1 Thessalonians 5:18 (KJV), *"In everything give thanks: for this is the will of God in Christ Jesus concerning you."*

We're not perfect, but we're pressing!

His "No" Is Still Love!

~

Why do we liken the answer "no" to being a bad thing? Our parents usually say no to protect us, often from paths they've already trod.

"No, you cannot play with that hot stove." "No, you cannot play outside after dark." "No, you cannot watch TV while doing your homework." Or "No, because I said so!"

We never know what the "no" is saving or protecting us from. God loves us so much, and He knows what's ahead. Every "no" is not to your detriment; some may be to keep you from dangers seen and unseen. When I was young, my adopted mom seemed to say no to everything. No to playing outside, no to sleepovers, no to having a boyfriend, and a big fat no to staying home from church—ever! But you know what? I am so grateful that she said no. I'm sure I avoided many bullets, headaches, and heartaches just because she wasn't afraid to tell me no.

God says "no" to cursing the Israelites. Numbers 22:12-14 (KJV) states, *"And God said unto Balaam, Thou shalt not go with them; thou shalt not curse the people: for they are blessed. And Balaam rose up in the morning, and said unto the princes of Balak, Get you into your land: for the Lord refuseth to give me leave to go with you. And the princes of Moab rose up, and they went unto Balak, and said, Balaam refuseth to come with us."* Here, when King Balak asked the prophet Balaam to curse the Israelites, God refused and blessed them, not once but thrice!

Another instance where God says no is found in 2 Corinthians 12:6-9 (KJV): *"For though I would desire to glory, I shall not be a fool; for I will say the truth: but now I forbear, lest any man should think of me above that which he seeth me to be, or that he heareth of me. And lest I should be exalted above measure through the abundance of the revelations, there was given to me a thorn in the flesh, the messenger of Satan to buffet me, lest I should be exalted above measure. For this thing I besought the Lord thrice, that it might depart from me. And he said unto me, My grace is sufficient for thee: for my strength is made perfect in weakness. Most gladly therefore will I rather glory in my infirmities, that the power of Christ may rest upon me."* Paul describes how God gave him a "thorn in his flesh" to keep him from becoming conceited. Paul pleads with God three times to remove it, but God refuses, saying, *"My grace is sufficient for you, for my power is made perfect in weakness."*

We often need a reminder of where we've been because we can become forgetful. Many haughty folks have forgotten where God has brought them from or what He has delivered them from. God is so gracious that He'll give us a limp to keep us from running away.

Jude 24-25 (Legacy Standard Bible) says, *"Now to Him who is able to keep you from stumbling, and to make you stand in the presence of His glory blameless with great joy, to the only God our*

Savior, through Jesus Christ our Lord, be glory, majesty, domin-
ion, and authority, before all time and now and forever.
Amen."

Christ's endeavor is for everyone to make it in, and sometimes that means telling us no. The enemy wants to sift us as wheat, but Christ comes so that we might have life and have it more abundantly.

John 10:10 (Berean Standard Bible): *"The thief comes only to steal and kill and destroy. I have come that they may have life and have it in all its fullness."*

There are so many snares and traps set for us that if God removed His hedge of protection, we'd be doomed! Sure, we experience trials and tribulations, but if you'd admit it, there are breaks between the blows. If the enemy had his way, he would devour us alive, but God says no.

I thank God that He doesn't allow us to run amok and that our Father loves us enough to say no!

It Isn't Meant to Destroy You, It's to Develop You

Colossians 2:6-7 (KJV) says, *"As ye have therefore received Christ Jesus the Lord, so walk ye in him: Rooted and built up in him, and stablished in the faith, as ye have been taught, abounding therein with thanksgiving."* Growth is a process! Nothing happens overnight. In everything you embark upon, it will take practice, tenacity, and strength to keep going. Don't let the first sign of resistance hinder your progress. In the end, you'll be glad that you kept going. Giving up is easy, but it won't be worth it! There is strength in stamina, stick-to-it-iveness, and patience if you keep going.

1 Peter 5:10 (KJV): *"But the God of all grace, who hath called us unto his eternal glory by Christ Jesus, after that ye have suffered a while, make you perfect, stablish, strengthen, settle you."*

Sometimes, there will be some suffering, but hold on! Sometimes, there will be heartaches, but keep going. Learn how to trust God in every situation. Trust God, not your friends, not your ability, but GOD.

Psalm 37:5 (KJV): *"Commit thy way unto the LORD; trust also in him; and he shall bring it to pass."*

You have to commit your way and your ways to the Lord. Commit your way to the Lord—your path, service, and life's journey. Your ways—your attitude, your habits, and your sinful desires. He will direct you if you trust Him. He will mature you if you let Him.

Jeremiah 17:7-8 (KJV): *"Blessed is the man that trusteth in the LORD, and whose hope the LORD is. For he shall be as a tree planted by the waters, and that spreadeth out her roots by the river, and shall not see when heat cometh, but her leaf shall be green; and shall not be careful in the year of drought, neither shall cease from yielding fruit."*

We have to learn to hang in there through any obstacle and remain confident in His leadership, resting on knowing what's best for us and what lies ahead. Even if it may seem uncertain today and concern is taking up too much space in your thoughts and emotions, remember God is already present tomorrow. The Bible gives us confidence that God is in control and has a plan. Furthermore, we can believe that God's plan is best for us.

Jeremiah 29:11 (KJV): *"For I know the thoughts that I think toward you, saith the LORD, thoughts of peace, and not of evil, to give you an expected end."*

It's nice knowing someone plans to do good things for you! You have a lot to look forward to! My birthday on March 8th, coinciding with International Women's Day, means everything to me. It's a day I greatly cherish, and my family and friends constantly make it special. However, when the Lord has plans for you that supersedes anything that anyone could ever do! You can count on it; you can go to sleep with a big grin, knowing that something great is coming!

Jeremiah 29:13-14 (KJV): *"And ye shall seek me, and find me, when ye shall search for me with all your heart. And I will be found of you, saith the LORD: and I will turn away your captivity, and I will gather you from all the nations, and from all the places whither I have driven you, saith the LORD; and I will bring you again into the place whence I caused you to be carried away captive."*

God wants good for you; no good thing will be withheld if you walk uprightly.

Allow God to Be Your Everything

P salms 119:57-58 (KJV) states, *"Thou art my portion, O LORD: I have said that I would keep thy words. I entreated thy favour with my whole heart: be merciful unto me according to thy word."*

In Tyler Perry's movie, "Diary of a Mad Black Woman," there's a scene where Cicely Tyson plays the mother of a daughter, Helen, whom her unfaithful and abusive husband has deeply hurt. On their 18th wedding anniversary, her husband physically removes her from their home for his paramour, Brenda. During this scene, as Helen cries to her mother, she says, "He was my everything!" Cicely Tyson responds, "God is your everything! And that God is a jealous God, and He would not have any other gods before Him." Helen had made her husband her everything, relying on him in ways that only God should be relied upon. This scene illustrates that people will fail you, but God will always come through. People may turn their backs on you, but God will never leave or forsake you.

Deuteronomy 31:6 (New International Version): *"Be strong and courageous. Do not be afraid or terrified because of them, for the LORD your God goes with you; He will never leave you nor forsake you."*

This is the kind of promise we need—one that we can count on, promises that won't get old, and someone who, no matter what comes or goes, won't change on us. God is a sustainer, a way maker, a comforter, a constant, a healer, a heart fixer, a mind regulator, and a heavy load bearer.

He tells us to cast our cares upon Him, for He cares for us. 1 Peter 5:7 (KJV): *"Casting all your care upon him; for he careth for you."* By putting and casting our worries on Him, we acknowledge our helplessness and desperate need for His guidance.

In my work with teenage girls, they often talk about needing substances, relationships, or other things to survive in this world. But I assure them that all they need is God. He will supply every need if they surrender to Him and align their will with His. Talk to God instead of reaching for a cell phone when lonely at night. When your pantry is bare, call on God. God is the answer—not the next fix, more income, or partner. He brings us joy and hope and is like a rock and shelter during difficult times. God can be there for you far greater than any relative, friend, or romantic partner.

Philippians 4:19 (KJV): *"But my God shall supply all your need according to his riches in glory by Christ Jesus."* Can you imagine someone supplying all of your needs? Whatever it is, they assure, "I've got it!" According to His riches in glory, the word states that's an immense amount!

Isaiah 41:10, 13 (KJV): *"Fear thou not; for I am with thee: be not dismayed; for I am thy God: I will strengthen thee; yea, I will help thee; yea, I will uphold thee with the right hand of my righteousness. For I the LORD thy God will hold thy right hand, saying unto thee, Fear not; I will help thee."*

Nothing is too hard for God; everything you need is in His hands. He wants to bless you, so let Him!

Deliverance Is in Your Praise

2 Chronicles 20:21-22 (KJV) states, *"And when he had consulted with the people, he appointed singers unto the LORD, and that should praise the beauty of holiness, as they went out before the army, and to say, Praise the LORD; for his mercy endureth forever. And when they began to sing and to praise, the LORD set ambushments against the children of Ammon, Moab, and mount Seir, which were come against Judah; and they were smitten."*

Have you ever met someone who feels like they always have to confront others themselves, never letting God handle the situation? Let me say this: You will never achieve deliverance if you focus more on your ego and less on God's will for your life. Sometimes, you may need help along the way, someone to hold you accountable, especially in areas where you're weak. My son LJ is my accountability partner. He helps me when my flesh needs to snap back at disrespectful people. My advice is not to linger in environments that keep you in that state of mind. What do you think the outcome will be if you're weak and continue to surround yourself with weakness?

I'm learning day by day that it's less about me and more about the path God has set me on. Sometimes, I find myself in tears, saying:

- I don't like it, but I'll do it.
- It seems stupid, but I'll say it.
- I'm often misunderstood, but I'll go.
- It gets lonely often, but God, I trust You.

My First Lady in Kentucky used to say, "You've got to trust Him even when you can't trace Him!" That's a true statement because sometimes it feels like God is nowhere to be found, but you've got to know He's there.

Job 14:14 (KJV) says, *"If a man die, shall he live again? all the days of my appointed time will I wait, till my change come."* The Message Bible says, "*All through these difficult days I keep hoping, waiting for the final change—for resurrection!"*

A transparent moment: my mother passed when I was two; she had nine brothers and sisters, and none of them wanted me. My adopted dad passed when I was nine; my daughter passed when I was eighteen. I've been in protective mode most of my life, thinking I needed to shield myself from further hurt. I'd cut people off. I didn't trust easily; if I did trust you and you hurt me, it would be over. However, God wants to deliver us and use us. God allows everything that happens to us, but it's not for us to become bitter; it's for us to become better. It's not for us to lash out.

1 Peter 5:10 (KJV) says, *"But the God of all grace, who hath called us unto his eternal glory by Christ Jesus, after that ye have suffered a while, make you perfect, stablish, strengthen, settle you."* You've got to see yourself as God sees you and look at people through the eyes of God.

Romans 5:8 (KJV): *"But God commendeth his love toward us, in that, while we were yet sinners, Christ died for us."* God gave us a chance even before we got it right.

Some may ask, "How can I smile while things are uncomfortable?" It's simple:

1. You have to die to your flesh.
2. You have to trust God to handle it.
3. You have to want Him to handle it.

This is where the praise comes from. You can praise God right in the middle of your problems because God's got you. You've got to learn to praise Him when you're down, when you're up, when you're broke, just as you do when you have a pocket full of money.

1 Thessalonians 5:18 (KJV) says, *"In every thing give thanks: for this is the will of God in Christ Jesus concerning you."* The Message translation says this: "Be cheerful no matter what; pray all the time; thank God no matter what happens. This is how God wants you who belong to Christ Jesus to live."

If you belong to Him, there ought to be something that separates you from the rest. You can always tell when someone is from New Jersey by their actions and speech; we talk loudly and expressively. New Orleanians have their distinct accent, and Floridians have their unique way of talking. Similarly, belonging to God should be evident in our behavior.

"Why don't you curse?" people ask me at work. "Because I'm representing God!" Why aren't you falling apart at every stumbling block? Because I belong to God, and I know He's got this!

James 1:1-4 (KJV) says, *"James, a servant of God and of the Lord Jesus Christ, to the twelve tribes which are scattered abroad, greeting. My brethren, count it all joy when ye fall into divers temptations; Knowing this, that the trying of your faith worketh patience. But let patience have her perfect work, that ye may be perfect and entire, wanting nothing."* Count it all joy, no matter the circumstance.

Deliverance is in your praise. And when we get that, we can always effectively and earnestly praise God.

It should be natural for you to praise God, whether you're up, down, in, or out. In Psalm 34, David reminds us to praise God through good times and bad. Praise should fill our hearts daily, no matter our circumstances–especially when walking through seasons of great trials. Get your praise on!

Deliverance is in your praise.

It Behooves You to Persevere

2 Corinthians 4:16-18 (KJV): *"For which cause we faint not; but though our outward man perish, yet the inward man is renewed day by day."*

No matter what things look like, we must keep going and never let the cares of the world cause us to turn away from God.

What does "behoove" mean? It is a duty or responsibility for someone to do something; it is incumbent on. It is also something that is appropriate or suitable; it befits.

Isaiah 40:31 (KJV): *"But they that wait upon the Lord shall renew their strength; they shall mount up with wings as eagles; they shall run, and not be weary; and they shall walk, and not faint."*

Waiting on the Lord renews your strength, builds character, and shows God, you trust Him.

What else does waiting on God do?

1. It gives you hope.
2. It builds endurance.
3. It increases your faith.
4. It allows you to see God operating in His element.

Waiting can be so difficult that it almost seems unachievable. Every item on our list has a time, plans, and goals, and we expect every action to lead to a successful outcome. Unfortunately, things don't always work out as planned. When we make our lists of goals, we often overlook the most crucial element, the Creator. Excluding God from our goals and aspirations may cause them to remain unmet. There is never a guarantee that everything will turn out as expected because God knows what we need, and things will work according to His plan.

Isaiah 55:8-9 (New King James Version): *"For My thoughts are not your thoughts, nor are your ways My ways, says the Lord. For as the heavens are higher than the earth, so are My ways higher than your ways, and My thoughts than your thoughts."*

God does not think like we do nor handle situations as we do. Where we may snap or feel like we should avenge someone, God says, "Let Me handle it." When we repay people, we often mess things up, but when God does it, it's divine.

In the between times and on the mountaintop, our life story should glorify God. We ought to set an example of what waiting on God looks like. Waiting on God pays off, showing the world that you trust God and are confident that "He is" just what the Word says He is.

What does it mean to persevere? It means to continue in a course of action, even in the face of difficulty or with little or no prospect of success. Holding tight and persevering in the face of hardships and adversity is essential to achieving God's ultimate salvation. It is strongly related to the concept of hope.

2 Chronicles 15:7 (KJV): *"Be ye strong therefore, and let not your hands be weak: for your work shall be rewarded."*

Hang on! Don't give up! PUSH past this! You've got what it takes; don't let the enemy tell you otherwise. You have a lot riding on this one! Your loved ones depend on you! Your breakthrough is just around the corner.

It behooves you to persevere! You've got this!

The Belief

I Samuel 1:17-20 (KJV) reads, *"Then Eli answered and said, Go in peace: and the God of Israel grant thee thy petition that thou hast asked of him. And she said, Let thine handmaid find grace in thy sight. So the woman went her way, and did eat, and her countenance was no more sad. And they rose up in the morning early, and worshipped before the LORD, and returned, and came to their house to Ramah: and Elkanah knew Hannah his wife; and the LORD remembered her. Wherefore it came to pass, when the time was come about after Hannah had conceived, that she bare a son, and called his name Samuel, saying, Because I have asked him of the LORD."*

Belief is an acceptance that a statement is true, or something exists, or it can be a firmly held opinion or conviction. So, essentially, it's about having faith in something, or as my husband often refers to it, your belief system. Hebrews 11:6 (The Message translation) says, *"It's impossible to please God apart from faith. And why? Because anyone who wants to approach God must believe both that He exists and that He cares enough to respond to those who seek Him."*

Hebrews 11:1 (The Expanded Translation) states, *"Faith means being sure of the things we hope for and knowing that something is real even if we do not see it."*

This means that I can and do trust God, even when I can't trace Him. We often go through situations where we feel God is nowhere to be found. However, faith and feelings don't mix. You may not feel Him, but He's there. Psalms 139:8 (KJV) says, *"If I ascend up into heaven, thou art there: if I make my bed in hell, behold, thou art there."* No matter what or where God is with us.

When I was pregnant with my eldest son Rey'chaun, a prophet called me out at a church service and said, "This son, which I didn't know I was having at the time, that you're carrying is going to be blessed." I believed what was being said to me, but I didn't know that I would have to refer to those words, "He's going to be blessed!" 1 Corinthians 13:9 (KJV) says, *"For we know in part, and we prophesy in part."* This means everything will not be revealed when you're prophesied to, so you must trust and believe God.

Long story short, Rey was born a month early and was an absolute blessing. Day 1, I enjoyed him, held him, and it was amazing. But on Day 2, doctors told me that my baby was born with a hole in his heart and had a rare disease called Tetralogy of Fallot, with a life expectancy of up to 30 years. From six months on, he began having surgery after surgery. But what carried me through was the prophecy, "This son is going to be blessed." And guess what? Today, my son is 32 years old!

In the scripture above, Hannah was saddened for years because she had no children. She had to watch Penninah, her husband's other wife, with her sons while she remained child-less. But Hannah kept going to God, diligently seeking Him.

Around the 19th verse of the chapter, Elkanah had relations with Hannah, and she became pregnant, which was evidence of things not seen. Before the year was out, Hannah gave birth to a son and named him Samuel, explaining, "I asked God for him."

You see, most times, it's more about the lesson than the blessing. She had a son, but the lesson was that she believed God. You might look at your good job, but God is trying to get you to see that you weren't qualified, but because you trusted Him to do it, He did it. Because you leaned and depended on Him, He made a way out of no way. Because you didn't veer to the left, God closed the mouths of your naysayers. Because you kept saying, "By His stripes, I am healed," He healed your body, and even the doctors were amazed. And because Job trusted God and didn't curse Him, He gave him double.

Whatever the thing is, stay before the Lord, put your trust in Him, and believe God.

John 14:14 (KJV) says, *"If ye shall ask any thing in my name, I will do it."*

"Do Better"

I Corinthians 13:1-7 (The Message Translation) reads, *"If I speak with human eloquence and angelic ecstasy but don't love, I'm nothing but the creaking of a rusty gate. If I speak God's Word with power, revealing all his mysteries and making everything plain as day, and if I have faith that says to a mountain, 'Jump,' and it jumps, but I don't love, I'm nothing. If I give everything I own to the poor and even go to the stake to be burned as a martyr, but I don't love, I've gotten nowhere. So, no matter what I say, what I believe, and what I do, I'm bankrupt without love."*

God wants to complete and establish you; He's created you for greatness. Sometimes, He wants more for us than we want for ourselves. 1 Corinthians 1:8-9 (The Amplified Version) says, *"And He will also confirm you to the end [keeping you strong and free of any accusation, so that you will be] blameless and beyond reproach in the day [of the return] of our Lord Jesus Christ."* Not only does He ask us to keep His commandments, but He also helps us to keep them.

I was at work the other day, and the history teacher, whom no one liked, was giving the students a test. He went over the test beforehand, then wrote some hints on the board and left them there during the test. But these stubborn, stiff-necked individuals still wouldn't take the teacher's help because they didn't like him, so most failed.

Isn't that like us? He left us a guidebook to follow, and some of us still won't accept the help. Jude 1:24 says, *"Now to Him who is able to keep you from stumbling or falling into sin, and to present you unblemished [blameless and faultless] in the presence of His glory with triumphant joy and unspeakable delight."* The problem is we're trying to save ourselves, doing everything without God. Then, when we get ourselves into trouble, we want to call on Him.

Before the crisis, it's often:

- "I'll pray later!"
- "I'm too tired to go to church today!"
- Or the big one, "God knows my heart!"

Ecclesiastes 5:5-6 (KJV) says, *"Better is it that thou shouldest not vow, than that thou shouldest vow and not pay. Suffer not thy mouth to cause thy flesh to sin; neither say thou before the angel, that it was an error: wherefore should God be angry at thy voice, and destroy the work of thine hands?"* Psalm 19:14 (KJV) adds, *"Let the words of my mouth, and the meditation of my heart, be acceptable in thy sight, O LORD, my strength, and my redeemer."*

Why, then, should we expect God to accept the negative things that come out of our mouths? Lies, cursing, backbiting, slander, gossip–how can these please Him? James 3:10 (KJV) states, *"Out of the same mouth proceedeth blessing and cursing.*

My brethren, these things ought not so to be." Is God pleased with your conversation? Ephesians 4:30 (KJV) advises, *"And grieve not the holy Spirit of God, whereby ye are sealed unto the day of redemption."*

God guarantees our salvation. Even some patented creations, though stamped and signed, are still faulty, but not so with God's promises. If He says it, you can believe it. John 3:16 (KJV) declares, *"For God so loved the world, that he gave his only begotten Son, that whosoever believeth in him should not perish, but have everlasting life."* He sacrificed His Son so that we might live, yet some of us struggle to give up sin to gain everlasting life. Your sin does not compare to His Son's sacrifice.

Galatians 2:21 (KJV) states, *"I do not frustrate the grace of God: for if righteousness come by the law, then Christ is dead in vain."* We should be grateful for His grace. Many of us would face severe consequences if the law judged our righteousness. His grace and mercy are the reasons we are still here today. Let's recap:

- If our words are acceptable to Him, He will strengthen and redeem us.
- If we believe in Him, we shall not perish.
- If we trust Him, He will direct our paths.

It's a fair exchange, considering He's not asking anyone to give up a child.

Do You Recognize His Voice?

John 10:27-28 (KJV) says, *"My sheep hear my voice, and I know them, and they follow me: And I give unto them eternal life; and they shall never perish."* God knows His sheep, and it is His endeavor that every one of us makes it in. But to do so, you've got to keep His commandments, live life according to His word, and allow Him to order your steps.

Revelation 21:27 (not Revelations 12:27) says, *"And there shall in no wise enter into it anything that defileth, neither whatsoever worketh abomination, or maketh a lie: but they which are written in the Lamb's book of life."* Is your name in there? Don't answer! That's a rhetorical question, meant to provoke thought.

Hebrews 4:12 (KJV): *"For the word of God is quick, and powerful, and sharper than any two-edged sword, piercing even to the dividing asunder of soul and spirit, and of the joints and marrow, and is a discerner of the thoughts and intents of the heart."* His word should pierce your heart, convict you, and enable you to hear His voice over Satan's schemes and tactics.

Psalms 34:8 (KJV): *"O taste and see that the LORD is good: blessed is the man that trusteth in him."* This verse means we are meant to fully experience the goodness of the Lord–His love, grace, and mercy. But we must obey Him.

John 10:1-5 (The Message Translation) states, *"Let me set this before you as plainly as I can. If a person climbs over or through the fence of a sheep pen instead of going through the gate, you know he's up to no good—a sheep rustler! The shepherd walks right up to the gate. The gatekeeper opens the gate to him and the sheep recognize his voice. He calls his own sheep by name and leads them out. When he gets them all out, he leads them and they follow because they are familiar with his voice. They won't follow a stranger's voice but will scatter because they aren't used to the sound of it."* Like a child who recognizes their mother's voice amid the noise, the more time you spend with the Lord, the more you will recognize His voice.

John 5:19 (ESV): *"So Jesus said to them, 'Truly, truly, I say to you, the Son can do nothing of his own accord, but only what he sees the Father doing. For whatever the Father does, that the Son does likewise."* When you belong to Christ, you will mimic His doings because you are His child. It will be evident whom you are following.

Romans 8:16 (KJV): *"The Spirit itself beareth witness with our spirit, that we are the children of God."* Just as family members share similarities in speech and mannerisms, Christians reflect Christ in their actions and character.

Continuing with the concept of family resemblance, if you are part of the Smith family, for example, you will probably exhibit similar behaviors and characteristics—your speech, your mannerisms, and so on. When you spend a lot of time with someone or are part of a family, you naturally adopt certain traits from them. This is often why someone might say you resemble your mother or behave like your father.

In the same way, Christians are called to act like Christ. This isn't about a physical resemblance but about adopting the behaviors, attitudes, and actions that reflect Christ's love and teachings. The more time we spend with Him, the more we understand and emulate His ways. Our actions, speech, and choices should reflect our spiritual family and lineage. This is at the heart of what it means to recognize and respond to His voice–to be guided by the example He set for us and to live in a way that honors that legacy.

Positioned with Purpose

S ometimes, we must position ourselves to receive what God has for us. Often, we're tired from working, doing, and going, so we make up an excuse to stay home from church. That very excuse might have cost you your Boaz.

Let me be transparent with you. One day, while on Facebook, a list of people "I might know" appeared on my timeline. My now-husband was one of them. I sent him a friend request because he was a friend of my spiritual dad and a member on my jurisdiction's page. That's all I did! Later that evening, he sent me a message. I consulted my spiritual father about him, and he shared some great things about my now-husband of almost eleven years!

This story illustrates that sometimes you have to position yourself to get blessed. Boaz would never have known who Ruth was had she not gone and lain at his feet. Ruth 3:6-10 (KJV) says, *"And she went down unto the floor, and did according to all that her mother in law bade her. And when Boaz had eaten and drunk, and his heart was merry, he went to lie down at the end of the heap of corn: and she came softly, and uncovered his feet, and laid her down. And it came to pass at midnight, that the man was afraid, and turned himself: and, behold, a woman lay at his feet. And he said, Who art thou? And she answered, I am Ruth thine handmaid: spread therefore thy skirt over thine handmaid; for thou art a near kinsman. And he said, Blessed be thou of the LORD, my daughter: for thou hast shewed more kindness in the latter end than at the beginning, inasmuch as thou followedst not young men, whether poor or rich."*

Sometimes, you need to get off the couch or porch, go sit at the mall, and read a book on one of the benches. Stop going out in headscarves, bonnets, hair rollers, and Walmart pajamas. Dress decently—you never know whom you'll run into.

Proverbs 31:10 (Evangelical Heritage Version) says, *"Who can find a wife with strong character? Her value is greater than that of gems."* Character is the quality of being individual in an interesting or unusual way, not just average, mediocre, or looking like everyone else. Strive to be extraordinary, never just average. He's looking for something different, someone who stands out. Walk on purpose, live on purpose, and position yourself with purpose.

Romans 8:28 (KJV): *"And we know that all things work together for good to them that love God, to them who are the called according to his purpose."* Therefore, if it's according to "His" purpose, we know things should be done excellently.

You were created to stand out, not fit in. Be someone who can be recognized in a crowd. 1 Peter 2:9 (NIV) states, *"But you are a chosen people, a royal priesthood, a holy nation, God's special possession, that you may declare the praises of him who called you out of darkness into his wonderful light."* As someone chosen by God, handpicked and set apart, everything about you should differ from the rest. Your conversation, your walk, the way you live, and the way you represent Christ should show a distinction between you and those around you.

It should be said, "There's just something about that [insert your name]!" My mother used to advise me, "Don't show them everything; leave some room for the imagination." What is it about her that is so intriguing? That makes people want to know her.

1 Corinthians 6:20 (KJV) reminds us, *"For ye are bought with a price: therefore glorify God in your body, and in your spirit, which are God's."* You are someone significant, and don't let anyone tell you differently. Be you, but with a purpose.

Pushing with Power

Isaiah 41:10 (The Message Bible) conveys a powerful message: *"Don't panic. I'm with you. There's no need to fear for I'm your God. I'll give you strength. I'll help you. I'll hold you steady, keep a firm grip on you."*

Today, I want to be transparent. I'm at a point in my life where I dread disturbances to my peace. After enduring enough pain, heartache, drama, and loss, I find myself panicking at the slightest hint of these recurring. I get emotional because I know God has called me to more than this, yet people's actions and agendas scare me. I fear acting contrary to His word. But I hear God reassuring me, "Don't worry about the people. You do what I've called you to do, and I'll handle the rest." He assures me I don't need to be nervous or on edge because He is in my corner.

Jude 1:18-21 (KJV) addresses the end times, showing that scoffers who delight in evil will come. It says, *"How that they told you there should be mockers in the last time, who should walk after their own ungodly lusts. These be they who separate themselves, sensual, having not the Spirit. But ye, beloved, building up yourselves on your most holy faith, praying in the Holy Ghost, Keep yourselves in the love of God, looking for the mercy of our Lord Jesus Christ unto eternal life."* We must build our lives upon our faith, pray in the Holy Spirit's power, and stay within God's love.

We must stand firm against temptation and testing, recognizing it as the enemy's tactics. Luke 10:19 (KJV) says, *"Behold, I give unto you power to tread on serpents and scorpions, and over all the power of the enemy: and nothing shall by any means hurt you."* Use your God-given authority to maintain peace, walk away, and resist the devil.

James 4:7 (The Living Bible) advises, *"So give yourselves humbly to God. Resist the devil and he will flee from you."* I promptly shut it down when engaged in an argument, saying, "I'm not arguing with anyone!" Develop a personal mantra or strategy to combat the enemy.

Some additional strategies for this journey include:

1. A strong prayer life.
2. Using affirmations of faith like, "God will fight my battles; I can do this."
3. Reading the Word and spending more time with God than with people.
4. Refusing to engage in foolishness.

Philippians 4:6 (The Living Bible) advises, *"Don't worry about anything; instead, pray about everything; tell God your needs, and don't forget to thank him for his answers."* Rely on God for help in daily life; we are powerless without Him. He is the source of our strength and power.

Titus 2:7-10 (The Message) states, *"But mostly, show them all this by doing it yourself, trustworthy in your teaching, your words solid and sane. Then anyone who is dead set against us, when he finds nothing weird or misguided, might eventually come around."*

Your actions can influence others. Through the Holy Spirit within us, we can affect people. As Christians and born leaders, we must represent Christ unequivocally and without doubt. The world should see the difference in us. Regardless of what comes our way, who acts contrary, or the challenges we face, we can push through.

- Push through obstacles.
- Push through appearances.
- Push through the most difficult times.

You possess the power to push. This power isn't just about overcoming external challenges; it's also about internal strength and resilience. It's about standing firm in your faith, upholding your convictions, and moving forward with the confidence that God is guiding and supporting you every step. Remember, the power to push through isn't just for your benefit; it's also a testament to those around you of the strength and steadfastness that comes from a life rooted in faith.

God Has the Final Say

Jeremiah 29:11-13 (KJV) states, *"For I know the thoughts that I think toward you, saith the Lord, thoughts of peace, and not of evil, to give you an expected end. Then shall ye call upon me, and ye shall go and pray unto me, and I will hearken unto you. And ye shall seek me, and find me, when ye shall search for me with all your heart."*

Have you ever encountered someone who thought they controlled your destiny? They might think, "If I cut them off, they'll have nothing," or "If I don't support their endeavors, they won't succeed." God allows certain people to walk out of our lives because they aren't conducive to our growth. Often, we cling to things and individuals that hold us back. We might have been further along in our journey if we had let go sooner.

God had a plan for your life before you were even born. Jeremiah 1:5 (KJV) says, *"Before I formed thee in the belly I knew thee; and before thou camest forth out of the womb I sanctified thee, and I ordained thee a prophet unto the nations."* You were destined for greatness, and no one else controls your destiny. We must remember not to give more power to people, places, and things than God. If your job shuts down or a relationship ends, why worry if we know God has the final say? Our provision comes from God alone.

My husband often says that God will send someone unexpected to bless you. Philippians 4:19 (KJV) reinforces this: *"But my God shall supply all your need according to his riches in glory by Christ Jesus."* Trust in God, not in people.

Despite having a smaller membership, we have never lacked in our ministry. God always supplies our needs and helps us meet our goals. Our church may not be large, but the unity and support of our members often make it seem as if we have a congregation of thousands. Some may have counted us out, thinking God's hand wasn't upon us, but He's been with us all along, proving to naysayers that He has the final say.

Isaiah 54:17 (KJV) states, *"No weapon that is formed against thee shall prosper; and every tongue that shall rise against thee in judgment thou shalt condemn. This is the heritage of the servants of the LORD, and their righteousness is of me, saith the LORD."* I've never been overly concerned with others' opinions of me. My stance has always been to question their significance in my life.

2 Corinthians 9:8 (KJV) says, *"And God is able to make all grace abound toward you; that ye, always having all sufficiency in all things, may abound to every good work."* This verse assures us that God provides for us in all situations so we can excel in our good works.

Our blessings come from above. James 1:17 (Living Bible) says, *"But whatever is good and perfect comes to us from God, the Creator of all light, and he shines forever without change or shadow."* God is consistent in His love and support, unlike others who may wish to see us fail.

3 John 1:2 (Berean Literal Bible) expresses a beautiful senti-ment: *"Beloved, I pray that in all respects you may prosper and be in good health, just as your soul prospers."* This verse reflects the comprehensive nature of God's care for us—it's not just about material or physical well-being but also the prosperity of our souls.

This chapter emphasizes the powerful truth that God, not people or circumstances, has the final say in our lives. He is the one who determines our path and provides for us. By trusting in God's plan and provision, we align ourselves with His will and open ourselves to the fullness of His blessings. Remem-ber, where others may fail or falter, God remains steadfast and true, guiding us towards our divine destiny.

God Has Not Forgotten You, It's Just Not Time Yet

Hebrews 6:10-15 (KJV) says, *"For God is not unrighteous to forget your work and labour of love, which ye have shewed toward his name, in that ye have ministered to the saints, and do minister. And we desire that every one of you do shew the same diligence to the full assurance of hope unto the end: That ye be not slothful, but followers of them who through faith and patience inherit the promises. For when God made promise to Abraham, because he could swear by no greater, he sware by himself, Saying, Surely blessing I will bless thee, and multiplying I will multiply thee. And so, after he had patiently endured, he obtained the promise."*

What promises are you waiting for? Have you ever placed something at the altar, Sunday after Sunday, reminding God of His promise? Have you woken up for early morning prayers, petitioning God for what He promised? Remember, God hasn't forgotten you; it's just not yet time. You may forget, but God is not forgetful. He is not senile or confused. It's simply not time yet.

Imagine if God gave us exactly what we wanted whenever we wanted it. Our faith wouldn't grow, nor would our trust be in God. We must remember who we are dealing with and who our Father is. If He gave us certain things too quickly, we might praise our jobs, credit, education, and ourselves instead of Him.

Sometimes circumstances must worsen so that only God can be credited for the turnaround. For example, He might allow financial struggles, so when you get that new car you didn't deserve, you'll credit Him, not your credit score. He might let a loved one reach death's door to give you a Lazarus experience. John 11:11 (KJV) says, *"Our friend Lazarus sleepeth; but I go, that I may awake him out of sleep."* The crowd thought Lazarus was dead, but to God, he was merely asleep.

Sometimes, God clears the room to bless you. Some people around you may not be ready for your next level. He's preparing to elevate you, but they can't go with you.

God might disrupt your circle to make you rely on Him, not people. Have you noticed when someone leaves your life, you start to rise? God couldn't bless you with finances because those around you would have drained it.

God knows what He's doing, and He knows you. He knows what you're ready for and what you can handle. He's heard conversations about you that you didn't hear. He knows who and what isn't for you.

You may feel at your end, but to God, you're just beginning. 1 Peter 5:10 (KJV) says, *"But the God of all grace, who hath called us unto his eternal glory by Christ Jesus, after that ye have suffered a while, make you perfect, establish, strengthen, settle you."*

You might think He forgot about you, but He was making something out of you, perfecting the purpose. I recall thinking about my son, who has been in jail for almost ten years, and saying, "He's not ready yet." Even when it's painful, God's timing is perfect. Proverbs 3:5-6 (KJV) advises, *"Trust in the LORD with all thine heart; and lean not unto thine own understanding. In all thy ways acknowledge him, and he shall direct thy paths."*

Sometimes, it seems like you're off course. You might wonder if you took a wrong turn or missed God's leading. But Romans 8:28 (KJV) assures us, *"And we know that all things work together for good to them that love God, to them who are the called according to his purpose."* He hasn't forgotten you; these things are part of the promise.

There might be pain, process, prolonging, or a pit before the promise, and sometimes you must push. But when you receive the promise, you'll forget that you ever thought God forgot you. God keeps His promises. 2 Corinthians 1:20 (KJV) states, *"For all the promises of God in him are yea, and in him Amen, unto the glory of God by us."*

We can't rush God; it's all in His timing. Job waited patiently (Job 14:14), Abraham and Sarah waited 25 years for Isaac (Genesis 12:4), Mary waited 30 years for Jesus to be revealed as the Messiah (Luke 2:22-40), Joseph waited 15 years to become overseer to the king (Genesis 41:46), and the woman with the issue of blood waited 12 years (Luke 8:43-48).

We rarely want to wait even 12 seconds. We want to keep reminding God of His promises, but He has not forgotten you. James 1:4 (KJV) says, *"But let patience have her perfect work, that ye may be perfect and entire, wanting nothing."*

You need to be equipped for this journey, fully trusting in God's timing and His perfect plan for your life.

Can God Choose You?

In Luke 1:26-30 (KJV), we read, *"And in the sixth month the angel Gabriel was sent from God unto a city of Galilee, named Nazareth, to a virgin espoused to a man whose name was Joseph, of the house of David; and the virgin's name was Mary. And the angel came in unto her, and said, Hail, thou that art highly favoured, the Lord is with thee: blessed art thou among women. And when she saw him, she was troubled at his saying, and cast in her mind what manner of salutation this should be. And the angel said unto her, Fear not, Mary: for thou hast found favour with God."* In verse 28, Mary is explicitly told she is favored by the Lord and set apart to deliver Jesus to Earth.

Mary was aware of the prophecy in Isaiah 7:14 (KJV), which says, *"Therefore the Lord himself shall give you a sign; Behold, a virgin shall conceive, and bear a son, and shall call his name Immanuel."* She had endeavored to live a moral life under the law, striving to please God. Was she faultless? No, she was human and likely made mistakes like anyone else, but God chose her for this exceptional role.

She was also endowed with the divine strength to endure the challenges of being Jesus' mother. The idea of her son being the Son of God would be hard to accept for those who didn't know her or understand God's plan. The very notion that she, a virgin, was pregnant would be scandalous and hard to believe. Yet God knew Mary would remain steadfast.

Now, reflect on yourself: Can God choose you? Can He rely on you to stand firm against ridicule, backlash, gossip, whispers, and pointing fingers? Unlike Mary, we might react defensively or confrontationally to such treatment. But Mary didn't have that option; she was chosen, considered, trusted, and given an assignment she didn't sign up for.

Reflecting on my experience, I recall working at MidAtlantic Youth Services. I was doing my job with no ambition for promotion, especially since I didn't meet the educational requirements. Yet, a supervisor saw my potential and chose me to supervise one of the most challenging dorms. With God's help and a resolute team, we turned the dorm around, making it a model for the facility.

This brings us back to Mary. Out of all the women in history, why was she chosen? Review the past week of your life. Consider each day: If it was an audition, did you give your best? If it was a test, did you pass? Did you glorify God from start to finish? There was a reason Mary was chosen–it wasn't a random draw from a hat. She must have been living in a way that suited her for this extraordinary role.

Ask yourself: Can God choose you? Are you living in a way that would make you a candidate for His purposes?

This Is Just a Scene, Not the Whole Story

2 Corinthians 4:8-9, 14 (CEV) states, *"We often suffer, but we are never crushed. Even when we don't know what to do, we never give up. In times of trouble, God is with us, and when we are knocked down, we get up again... because we know that God raised the Lord Jesus back to life. And just as God raised Jesus, he will also raise us to life. Then he will bring us into his presence together."* This is not the end; God isn't through with me yet. This is just a chapter, not the whole book. This is just a sip, not the entire cup. It's just a seed, not a tree. Just the blueprint...

Melvin Crispell wrote a song, "Not the End of the Story," and a few lyrics resonate during hard times: "Almost gave up in the middle of the night. Almost quit in the middle of the fight. Tryna find a way through the storms of life. But You said, 'Trust me, I've got this.' I really don't know where this road's gonna lead. Feeling all alone brings me down to my knees. Battling a storm, trying to find a little peace. But I feel Your presence, and You tell me it's not the end of your story."

I know this doesn't look like what was promised. And this trial doesn't match triumph, but every step is needed. Romans 8:28 (KJV) says, *"And we know that all things work together for good to them that love God, to them who are the called according to his purpose."* It will all work together in the end. The wiser saints would say, "You will understand it better by and by." I admit I'm one of those people who likes to fast forward to the end of a show, wanting to know everything that happens, scene by scene. I get mad at the TV, talk to it, get upset when characters die off, are replaced, or leave the story and return differently. I automatically assume I know how the story should end, but I'm not the writer, nor do we get to determine how this plays out. Hebrews 12:2 (Legacy Standard Bible) states, *"Fixing our eyes on Jesus, the author and perfecter of faith, who for the joy set before Him endured the cross, despising the shame, and has sat down at the right hand of the throne of God."*

Church people can label you based on one moment of your journey. You fall once or twice; now they're calling you a failure! You were on pills for one season; now you're an addict! They see you coming out of the local bar, and you're a club-hopper! (You might've just been picking up some wings... They do have the best wings.) But remember to tell them, "My whole life is not my one mistake!" God is not through with me yet! And only He gets to say how well I turn out.

I stopped using profanity in 1987. My goal was that when I had my first child, I didn't want to be cussing around her. When I run into someone in New Jersey, they'll first say, "I remember this and that... Peaches (my nickname) was a fighter and blah, blah, blah!" People will remind you of your past, won't they?

Don't base what Peaches did 36 years ago on the Daphanny that God is using mightily today! That was just a scene, not my whole story.

What Has God Called You To?

I Peter 2:9 (KJV) states, *"But ye are a chosen generation, a royal priesthood, an holy nation, a peculiar people; that ye should shew forth the praises of him who hath called you out of darkness into his marvellous light."* Often, we struggle to move forward because we are stuck in the past. In Genesis 19, Lot's wife became a pillar of salt after she looked back at Sodom.

Luke 9:62 (KJV) says, *"And Jesus said unto him, No man, having put his hand to the plough, and looking back, is fit for the kingdom of God."* You can't effectively move forward if you are looking backward. You will trip, as your eyes aren't on the goal and cannot see where you're going.

Isaiah 43:18-19 in The Message Bible expresses this thought beautifully: *"Forget about what's happened; don't keep going over old history. Be alert, be present. I'm about to do something brand-new. It's bursting out! Don't you see it? There it is! I'm making a road through the desert, rivers in the badlands."* God wants to bring you out and deliver you. He wants to heal your body, but you must stop declaring that you're sick.

Once, my mother-in-law, my husband, and I were watching Dr. Phil. The episode featured a young lady who was practically starving herself. She didn't want help or advice on healing; she just kept saying, "I'm sick, and I can't get well." Imagine how God feels after He died for our sins, was wounded for our transgressions, and endured a gruesome beating, only for us to ignore all that and still claim to be sick and doubt healing. Isaiah 53:5 (New American Standard Bible) says, *"But He was pierced for our offenses, He was crushed for our wrongdoings; The punishment for our well-being was laid upon Him, And by His wounds we are healed."*

You have to want to come out of what you're in to walk into what He's called you to. God has called you to so much more, but you may be comfortable in your current situation. Make the declaration that you will be all that He has called you to be.

Ask yourself, "What has God called me to?" Ephesians 2:10 (KJV) says, *"For we are his workmanship, created in Christ Jesus unto good works, which God hath before ordained that we should walk in them."* God has ordained you to do great things. Jeremiah 1:5 (KJV) says, *"Before I formed thee in the belly I knew thee; and before thou camest forth out of the womb I sanctified thee, and I ordained thee a prophet unto the nations."* So, then, why do we settle for mediocrity? Why do we desire a sad story when God has called us to major things, yet we operate in minor ones?

Notice I say "we" because this message hit me first. I often reflect on my early days in ministry. How I was a first lady before I officially became one, how people trusted me with their secrets, asked me to pray for them, and how God showed me things in the spirit. I used to say, "The danger in having me around was that I have the Holy Ghost."

Yet, I sometimes wonder, am I missing something now? God still shows me things, but am I as connected as I used to be? I had a vision of my eldest son in an orange jumpsuit before he was incarcerated and knew of a dear friend's passing before receiving the phone call. What has hindered me? What's different now? As God's people, we need to get back to our posts. God is calling us to greater work, and it's time to put aside excuses. We are missing out, and I include myself in this.

A dying world needs us, and we're holding back, denying others our gifts. God has invested in us so we can invest in the lives of others, but we are stagnant, lazy, and seem to have forgotten the sacrifice Christ made. We must remember how Christ was beaten. God gave His only begotten son so that whoever believes in Him should not perish but have everlasting life. It's time to stop sitting back.

1 Peter 2:9 (KJV) reminds us, *"But ye are a chosen generation, a royal priesthood, an holy nation, a peculiar people; that ye should shew forth the praises of him who hath called you out of darkness into his marvellous light."*

Sometimes, we act just like the world, as if we have no hope. Being rich in faith, we ought not to talk about being broke. So much is afforded to us simply because God is who He is. "Lazarus, come forth!" Insert your name: "_____, come forth!" Ministry, come forth! What has God called you to?

"He Didn't Call Us to Compete, He Called Us to Compel"

~

Galatians 6:4-5 (Legacy Standard Bible) instructs, *"But each one must examine his own work, and then he will have reason for boasting in regard to himself alone, and not in regard to another. For each one will bear his own load."*

Luke 14:23 (KJV) states, *"And the lord said unto the servant, Go out into the highways and hedges, and compel them to come in, that my house may be filled."*

In ministry, there is often a tendency towards competition: who has the biggest church, the most members, preaches better, drives a nicer car, dresses best, or impresses the Pastor more. But the real question is, who is winning souls for Christ? While many are concerned with frivolous matters, who is concerned about the lost?

In the Book of Hosea, the Lord commanded Hosea to marry a prostitute named Gomer. Despite her unfaithfulness and promiscuity, Hosea was instructed to bring her back home continually. This narrative symbolizes Israel's spiritual adultery with other gods and mirrors how Christ treats us. Despite our wanderings and worldly pursuits, God accepts us with open arms, even being described as married to the backslider. Jeremiah 3:14-15 (NKJV) affirms this: *"Return, O backsliding children," says the LORD; "for I am married to you. I will take you, one from a city and two from a family, and I will bring you to Zion. And I will give you shepherds according to My heart, who will feed you with knowledge and understanding."* He calls for our return, even in our unfaithfulness, and welcomes us with a clean heart.

In contrast, if we were to accept someone back, many of us would expect them to return begging with grand gestures of apology. Yet, here is God pleading for our return after all our rebellion and sin, and He is the one offering gifts.

Romans 12:2 (KJV) advises, *"And be not conformed to this world: but be ye transformed by the renewing of your mind, that ye may prove what is that good, and acceptable, and perfect, will of God."* We are called to follow the Lord's leading, allowing Him to transform our minds. Despite being betrayed, beaten, abused, and lied about, Jesus exemplified forgiveness, saying, *"Father, forgive them; for they know not what they do"* (Luke 23:34, KJV).

When Jesus knew Judas would betray Him, He did not leave the table but continued to dine with him. Matthew 26:21-23 (KJV) recounts, *"And as they did eat, he said, Verily I say unto you, that one of you shall betray me. And they were exceeding sorrowful, and began every one of them to say unto him, Lord, is it I? And he answered and said, He that dippeth his hand with me in the dish, the same shall betray me."* Could you, like Jesus, sit calmly, knowing betrayal was imminent? This is where you might hear your favorite cousin exclaim, "WOWWWWW!

They sat at your table! Ate your food!! And had the nerve to do that!! 'If I were you!!'"

In these moments, we often encounter friends offering advice that is not Christ-like. It's important to remember that our calling is not to compete with one another but to compel others to come to Christ. We should focus on fulfilling God's mission rather than getting entangled in worldly competitions and concerns.

Galatians 6:4-5 reminds us that we each have our work to examine and our own load to bear. It's about staying true to our calling, leading by example, and extending the same grace and forgiveness that Christ has shown us. We are called to be light and salt, compelling others through our actions, words, and lives to come into His marvelous light.

The Right Posture

Psalms 16:5-10 (The Message Bible) expresses a heartfelt choice and recognition: *"My choice is you, God, first and only. And now I find I'm your choice! You set me up with a house and yard. And then you made me your heir! The wise counsel God gives when I'm awake is confirmed by my sleeping heart. Day and night I'll stick with God; I've got a good thing going and I'm not letting go. I'm happy from the inside out, and from the outside in, I'm firmly formed. You canceled my ticket to hell—that's not my destination!"*

When people think about posture concerning Jesus, they often envision looking up. Abundant fruit comes when we assume the proper posture. The Safari dictionary defines posture as "A particular way of dealing with or considering something; an approach or attitude." You've probably heard the saying, "Your attitude determines your altitude."

Things may look bad, but it's how I go through it, consider it, and deal with it. If you lay in bed all day saying, "I'm sick," you'll feel sick and sad. However, if you get dressed, put on your best outfit, and say, "I'm going to walk this out," you can shift your focus. You see things differently and can cast your cares upon Him, for He cares for you and can heal you. Hebrews 11:6 (KJV) reinforces this, stating, *"But without faith it is impossible to please him: for he that cometh to God must believe that he is, and that he is a rewarder of them that diligently seek him."* Faith is the complete trust and confidence in someone or something.

Surround yourself with friends who encourage you to get out of bed, not those who let you languish there. You strengthen one another when you're in covenant with the right friends. It's all about how we can posture ourselves to help one another. Don't always be the one with your "hand out," your "back turned," or your "mouth always open."

Our posture makes all the difference. We must remember who God is and realize His power to change us and our surroundings. Sometimes, it just takes tweaking the things and people around you.

When I first moved to Pennsylvania, I became friends with a few people and hung out with certain ones. As time went on, God severed those connections. He allowed people to hurt and disappoint me so I could let go. I was devastated but realized that not everyone's posture matches mine. We can't fit together if we don't align with the right people.

We should remember that we are bought with a price, and our posture should always be built on His kingdom. Falling in love with Jesus was the best thing I've ever done because it taught me to lean on Him and depend on Him. Proverbs 3:5-6 (KJV) advises, *"Trust in the LORD with all thine heart; and lean not unto thine own understanding. In all thy ways acknowledge him, and he shall direct thy paths."* He can't direct your path if you're not postured correctly; you must be able to go if He tells you to go. You can't walk through the valley if you're sitting. Your attitude, mindset, and environment must be postured for action.

Think about how you were when you first met someone special. You wanted to spend time with them, talk to them, know about them. You postured yourself to listen to them. John 14:31 (KJV) says, *"But that the world may know that I love the Father; and as the Father gave me commandment, even so I do. Arise, let us go hence."* "Hence" means from this place. In this scripture, Jesus shows that the world needs to know he loves the Father and does exactly what the Father tells him to do. His model of humble spiritual posture brings us in step with the Spirit and into alignment with the Father's will.

This can alter our perspective. Hebrews 12:2 (KJV) says, *"Looking unto Jesus the author and finisher of our faith; who for the joy that was set before him endured the cross, despising the shame, and is set down at the right hand of the throne of God."* The Message Bible says, *"Keep your eyes on Jesus, who both began and finished this race we're in. Study how he did it. He never lost sight of where he was headed—that exhilarating finish in and with God. He could handle anything along the way: the cross, the shame, marital problems, money issues, whatever. And now he's there, in the place of honor, right alongside God."*

The right posture influences how you walk, talk, live, and think. Colossians 3:1-2 (KJV) says, *"If ye then be risen with Christ, seek those things which are above, where Christ sitteth on the right hand of God. Set your affection on things above, not on things on the earth."* The proper posture gives you the right attitude, leading to the right outcome.

How Grateful Are You?

Romans 5:6-8 (Living Bible) states, *"When we were utterly helpless, with no way of escape, Christ came at just the right time and died for us sinners who had no use for him. Even if we were good, we really wouldn't expect anyone to die for us, though, of course, that might be barely possible. But God showed his great love for us by sending Christ to die for us while we were still sinners."* Imagine someone trusting you with a million dollars without knowing you personally. Christ's sacrifice for us while we were sinners exemplifies trust and love beyond comprehension.

The Bible affirms God's omniscience and deep knowledge of us even before birth. It's astounding that He sacrificed for us despite our flawed nature–spoiled, stuck in our ways, or rebellious. Romans 6:1-3 (KJV) questions the continuation of sin, considering grace: *"Shall we continue in sin, that grace may abound? God forbid. How shall we, that are dead to sin, live any longer therein? Know ye not, that so many of us as were baptized into Jesus Christ were baptized into his death?"*

The Message Bible rephrases this as a call to leave behind our old life of sin and embrace a new life of grace. We're urged to let God transform us, following the ultimate example of Jesus, who forgave even in the face of betrayal.

My personal experience mirrors this teaching. Recently, I was angered by my husband's (the Pastor) response to a simple request. Inspired by a movie scene, I playfully asked him to bring home spaghetti sauce, only to be reminded of his long workday. My reaction was anger, yet I knew his tendency for post-work fatigue. I realized I allowed the enemy to stir my anger over a predictable response. God keeps allowing these situations to mature my responses and grow in grace.

Romans 8:28 (NIV) reminds us that *"all things work together for good to those who love God, to those who are called according to his purpose."* This should compel us to gratitude, recognizing Christ's sacrifice for us. How can we harbor resentment or lack compassion when Christ embraced us in our sinfulness?

After the spaghetti sauce incident, while my husband slept, God nudged me to apologize for my response. Romans 4:8 (AMP) encourages focusing on what is true, honorable, and right. I often express a desire to be with the Lord soon, yet my son LJ jokes that God won't take me yet because of my sharp tongue. While I've mastered positive thinking most of the time, it's that 20% when I dwell on negative thoughts that challenge me.

God allows us these moments to get our lives right. He permits us to err yet gives us warnings to correct our course. Isaiah 5:20 (KJV) pronounces woe upon those who confuse good with evil, highlighting the importance of discernment and gratitude.

In my work at the bank, following step-by-step instructions is crucial for opening accounts correctly. This parallels our spiritual journey; Christ has given us basic instructions and ignoring them leads to errors and warnings. It's our responsibility to correct these mistakes to ensure our spiritual accounts "export" correctly.

So, how grateful are you? Can you live for Him since He died for you? What are you doing for Him? Christ gave His life for us; what are we giving in return?

Thank God for the Cross

E phesians 2:11-13 (Living Bible) reminds us, *"Never forget that once you were heathen and that you were called godless and 'unclean' by the Jews. But now you belong to Christ Jesus, and though you once were far away from God, now you have been brought very near to him because of what Jesus Christ has done for you with his blood."*

When you reflect on the Cross, what comes to mind? Is it His death, the manner of His death, or that He died for us? The film "Passion of the Christ" offers a glimpse into the treatment and torment He endured. Jesus Christ, as the sacrificial lamb, took upon Himself the punishment we deserved, atoning for our sins and freeing us from the bondage of sin.

Romans 5:8 (KJV) says, *"But God commendeth his love toward us, in that, while we were yet sinners, Christ died for us."* The word "yet" implies a continuous state–while we still needed work. Christ died for us. Yet, many still struggle to grasp the magnitude of His sacrifice and remain disconnected from the deep connection He forged through His blood shed on the Cross.

Acts 17:28 reminds us we are His offspring, His children. The necessity of Christ's bloodshed for the remission of sins is affirmed in Hebrews 9:22, which states, *"And almost all things are by the law purged with blood; and without shedding of blood is no remission."*

His birth, life, and death were for us all while we were yet sinners. He didn't wait for us to get it right. The sacrifice of Christ enables us to live, a notion difficult for many to fully comprehend or accept. Mary, the mother of Jesus, understood the assignment and bore the weight of carrying a child destined to die for the world.

Taking up your cross means associating yourself with Christ and sharing in His rejection. Yet, many want to claim Christ without sharing in His sufferings. We often resist dying to our flesh and the sins that entangle us. But to truly understand His sacrifice, we must seek to know Him and be conformed to His death, as Paul expressed in Philippians 3:10 (New English Translation).

Killing the flesh from a spiritual perspective is akin to what Christ did on the cross. Ephesians 1:20 says, *"Which he wrought in Christ, when he raised him from the dead, and set him at his own right hand in the heavenly places."* We are called to do the same–to kill our flesh so we can have eternal life and one day live in Heaven.

John 3:16-17 (KJV) proclaims, *"For God so loved the world, that he gave his only begotten Son, that whosoever believeth in him should not perish, but have everlasting life. For God sent not his Son into the world to condemn the world; but that the world through him might be saved."* It's through Him we find salvation.

We can't do this without Him. Without Him, we can't live, breathe, move, or even exist. We are nothing without Him. His sacrifice on the Cross is what gives us life. He bore the sins of the world while we were still sinners. Because of His life, we can face tomorrow, live without fear, and find hope. It's "Because He Lives."

Thank God for the Cross. He gave Himself, sacrificed His life, and bore the sins of this world. If it had not been for the Lord on our side, it would have been daunting to think where we might be. It's His life, His sacrifice, that allows us to live. The Cross is not just a symbol of suffering; it is a testament to the ultimate sacrifice made of love for us. As believers, we owe our existence to the Cross and the hope it represents. Let us be ever grateful and never forget the price paid for our freedom and salvation. Thank God for the Cross.

Lord, Help Me Walk in "Your" Spirit and Not "My" Flesh

Galatians 5:16-17 advises, *"I say then: Walk in the Spirit, and you will not fulfill the lust of the flesh. For the flesh lusts against the Spirit, and the Spirit against the flesh; and these are contrary to one another, so that you do not do the things that you wish."* This scripture highlights the constant struggle between our spiritual aspirations and earthly desires.

Have you ever considered how we are influenced by what we consume, whether medication, food, or other substances? Just like how these external factors affect our physical state, our spiritual condition is influenced by what we internalize spiritually. If we immerse ourselves in prayer and Scripture, we will be led by the Spirit rather than our flesh.

Often, we find ourselves walking in the flesh rather than in faith. We seek visible paths and tangible results, but faith requires us to relinquish control and trust in Christ's guidance. It's about stepping into the unknown, trusting in provision despite scarcity, and believing in fulfillment before it manifests.

Our fleshly nature can lead us astray, as Romans 7:18-20 (NIV) stated: *"I know that nothing good lives in me, that is, in my sinful nature. I want to do what is right, but I can't... It is sin living in me that does it."* This highlights the importance of relying on the Lord's guidance since our fleshly inclinations can often lead us away from what is right.

The advice we receive from worldly sources, like our parents or peers, may be well-intentioned but not aligned with biblical teachings. For instance, worldly advice might be about self-preservation. In contrast, the Bible teaches us to love unconditionally, even those who may misuse our kindness.

In dealing with betrayal or misuse, we should remember Christ's example. He knew Judas would betray Him, yet He continued to show him love and shared a meal with him. We mustn't be so focused on protecting ourselves that we lose sight of our spiritual mission. God watches over us, so we should persist in doing good, as Romans 12:21 (KJV) urges, *"Be not overcome of evil, but overcome evil with good."*

The lyrics from Kirk Franklin's song, "Order My Steps," resonate deeply during times of prayer: "Bridle my tongue, let my words edify... Order my steps in your word." Such guidance is crucial for leading a life in harmony with God's will.

Where would we be without God's direction? We must remain steadfast in our faith, ensuring our names are inscribed in the Lamb's Book of Life. I often say, "Life is short, and then you die!" We must be prepared for the moment our name is called.

Don't Let the Enemy Take You Down with Him

Revelation 20:1-3 (NKJV) narrates a powerful vision: *"Then I saw an angel coming down from heaven, having the key to the bottomless pit and a great chain in his hand. He laid hold of the dragon, that serpent of old, who is the Devil and Satan, and bound him for a thousand years; and he cast him into the bottomless pit, and shut him up, and set a seal on him, so that he should deceive the nations no more till the thousand years were finished. But after these things he must be released for a little while."*

Recalling a family dinner, I remember when my youngest, then around four, began tilting back in his chair. Despite warnings, he persisted, finding amusement in the risk. Inevitably, his chair toppled, pulling his sister down with him in a comical yet cautionary scene. This incident mirrors our spiritual journey: ignoring warnings can lead to unintended consequences.

I John 2:1-5 underscores this: *"My little children, I am writing these things to you so that you may not sin. But if anyone does sin, we have an advocate with the Father, Jesus Christ the right-*

eous." It's a reminder to heed the Lord's commandments, as the path to salvation lies in obedience. John 14:15 (ESV) reinforces this: *"If you love me, you will keep my commandments."*

Satan's influence is pervasive and destructive. As believers, we must be vigilant, understanding his objective to derail us. John 10:10 (NLT) contrasts this with Christ's promise: "The thief comes only to steal and kill and destroy. I came that they may have life and have it abundantly."

Obedience to God is a cornerstone of our faith, challenging us to trust and follow His directives. Biblical narratives provide timeless insights and guidance, essential for navigating life's complexities.

Ephesians 4:23-24 (TLB) encourages transformation: *"Now your attitudes and thoughts must all be constantly changing for the better. Be a new and different person, holy and good. Clothe yourself with this new nature."* Our optimistic or pessimistic attitude shapes our perspective and witness as Christians.

Embrace a 'Christimist' viewpoint, focusing on the promises and strength found in Scripture. Psalms 18:32 (KJV) states, *"It is God that girdeth me with strength, and maketh my way perfect."* This perspective aligns us with God's purpose, enabling us to resist the enemy's attempts to drag us down.

Remember, the enemy's goal is to ensure we miss Heaven as he did. Resist becoming his prodigy; instead, aspire to be a part of God's royal priesthood.

The Woman Within Me

Luke 2:36-38 introduces us to Anna, a prophet of notable commitment and devotion: *"There was also a prophet, Anna, the daughter of Penuel, of the tribe of Asher. She was very old; having lived with her husband seven years after her marriage, and then was a widow until she was eighty-four. She never left the temple but worshiped night and day, fasting and praying. Coming up to them at that very moment, she gave thanks to God and spoke about the child to all who were looking forward to the redemption of Jerusalem."*

Anna epitomizes the ideal Christian disciple, dedicated to sharing the gospel, fasting, and constant prayer. Her life is an example for us, challenging us to trust wholly in the Lord. As the only named female prophet in the New Testament, Anna's devoutness and commitment to prayer in the temple showcase her extraordinary faith.

Each of us harbors a prophetess, missionary, teacher, and more. My journey as a First Lady was preceded by doing the Lord's work—praying, being entrusted with sensitive information, visiting the sick, and giving my time. There's ample work in God's kingdom, which calls for active participation.

Where are today's women of such vigor and dedication? Who is rising early to seek God, visiting the fainthearted, and fulfilling the commission to serve the Lord? Committing to God means surrendering all control and seeking His will, engaging daily with the Scripture, and being prepared to obey Him.

It's vital to remain zealous and dynamic in our faith. Romans 12:11 encourages us, *"Do not let your zeal subside; keep your spiritual fervor, serving the Lord."* Be enthusiastic for Christ, unwavering in your commitment, and embody the true woman of God.

Who is the woman within you? Is she fully active? Does she reach out to others? What's holding you back? Matthew 9:35-38 reminds us of Jesus' compassion and calls for laborers in His harvest, urging us to be proactive in His work.

Our commitment to God's work must be unwavering regardless of challenges or skepticism. Ecclesiastes 9:10 (NASB) advises, *"Whatever your hand finds to do, do it with all your might; for there is no activity, planning, knowledge, or wisdom in Sheol where you are going."*

Ignite the powerful fire within you. Discover and embrace your true self, rise, and step forth boldly. Whether it's being a great mother, an exceptional wife, a successful business owner, or any dream you hold, God has equipped you for greatness. Success lies in action; failure in inaction. Chase your dreams, for only then can they become a reality.

Salvation Out Loud

S ince 2005, I have worked within the legal system, holding positions in maximum security prisons, county jails, and juvenile detention centers worldwide. Each day, I resolved to maintain a good and Godly standard. When a sergeant remarked, "You don't swear? Before it's over, you will!" I was determined to prove him wrong. I wanted to look and sound different from those who had passed through those doors. Representing my God without compromise was a choice and a conviction that came naturally.

My salvation is paramount, and my every endeavor is to live it out loud. Accepting Christ meant embracing His attributes, characteristics, and standards, leaving no room for negotiation of His word. The misconception that one can serve God in any manner is dangerous. The Bible provides explicit instructions on how to conduct ourselves, live our lives, and treat others. God seeks earnest and truthful servants with the conviction to stand firm in their beliefs, unswayed even by the gravest threats.

Romans 14:8-10 (KJV) underscores this, stating, *"For whether we live, we live unto the Lord; and whether we die, we die unto the Lord: whether we live therefore, or die, we are the Lord's."* This scripture emphasizes that our primary aim should be to live for the Lord, in life and death, recognizing that we belong to Him.

The story of Shadrach, Meshach, and Abednego in Daniel 3:28-30 demonstrates the power of unwavering faith. Their refusal to bow to any god other than the true and living God, even under the threat of a fiery death, not only saved them but also led to their promotion by Nebuchadnezzar. This narrative teaches Christians the importance of being prepared to serve the Lord with their lives, regardless of the circumstances.

Philippians 1:21 (KJV) states, *"For to me to live is Christ, and to die is gain."* This conveys the notion that our entire lives should be dedicated to Christ. Living for Christ means illuminating the world and bringing others into God's kingdom; paradoxically, death is seen as a gain in this context.

Philippians 2:4-5 instructs, *"Each of you should be concerned not only about your own interests, but about the interests of others as well. You should have the same attitude toward one another that Christ Jesus had."* As we serve God, our actions and speech should align with Christ's example, showing love not out of obligation but with genuine desire. Our primary goal should be to emulate Christ in our actions and words.

We need to channel the same energy we had before accepting Christ into our current endeavors, like prayer meetings, women's teachings, and feeding the poor. Often, we become so absorbed in our own lives that we neglect these crucial aspects of service. It's time to reengage and serve God with the same vigor and passion we once had for worldly pursuits.

My Finite Mind

The concept of the finite mind, attributed to John Williams, recognizes the human mind's limited capacity. Finite implies having limits or boundaries, an end or a limit. This concept is echoed in Mark 9:24 (MEV): *"Immediately the father of the child cried out with tears, 'Lord, I believe. Help my unbelief!'"* This plea reflects our struggle to maintain faith amidst overwhelming circumstances.

Why do we confine God to a box? Why don't we always have the faith in Him we should? God grants a measure of faith to everyone, which serves as a foundation for further faith development. Our faith is a journey, beginning with what God initially instills in us.

John 14:13-14 says, *"And whatsoever ye shall ask in my name, that will I do, that the Father may be glorified in the Son. If ye shall ask anything in my name, I will do it."* Faith connects us and God's power, enabling believers to act confidently, knowing their prayers are heard.

Change your mindset and your speech. If you desire something, ask God. He delights in blessing you. Proverbs 21:1
(Living Bible) illustrates God's influence: *"Just as water is
turned into irrigation ditches, so the Lord directs the king's
thoughts. He turns them wherever he wants to."* This means if
God can influence a king, He can certainly influence our lives.

Romans 8:31 reinforces this: *"If God is for us, who can be
against us?"* This scripture empowers us to believe we can
accomplish anything with God on our side.

Psalm 50:10 is often quoted to illustrate God's omnipotence:
*"For every beast of the forest is mine, the cattle on a thousand
hills."* This verse symbolizes God's dominion over all earthly
riches, encouraging us to trust His provision.

So, why do we sometimes hesitate to trust Him fully? We
often let our perceived limitations–like lack of education,
experience, or financial resources–overshadow our faith. But
with God, these limitations are irrelevant. He is capable of far
more than we can comprehend. Romans 11:33 (Modern
English Version) says, *"O the depth of the riches and wisdom
and knowledge of God! How unsearchable are His judgments
and unfathomable are His ways!"* This reminds us of the infi-
nite scope of God's power and wisdom.

Matthew 16:8 (KJV) cautions against doubt: *"O ye of little
faith, why reason ye among yourselves, because ye have brought
no bread?"* This highlights our tendency to rely on our understanding rather than God's providence.

We trust God is bigger than any challenge we face, including
health crises like cancer. His power exceeds our wildest dreams
and imaginations. We need to align our thinking with the
magnitude of His might and capability.

Let's shift our mindset to trust God's boundless power and grace fully. He's not just mighty; He's the epitome of greatness. Remember, God owns the entire galaxy–our challenges are small in comparison. Let God lead and watch Him work wonders.

Lord Help Me Keep My Word

Ecclesiastes 5:5 (KJV) states: *"Better is it that thou shouldest not vow, than that thou shouldest vow and not pay."* The Living Bible Translation phrases it as: *"It is far better not to say you'll do something than to say you will and then not do it."* The Message Bible simplifies it further: *"When you tell God you'll do something, do it—now. God takes no pleasure in foolish drivel. Vow it, then do it. Far better not to vow in the first place than to vow and not pay up."*

This suggests that keeping your word rather than making a commitment you cannot fulfill is preferable. It is essential to honor our promises and obligations. Still, it is wiser to avoid making them if we are uncertain about our ability to deliver. A promise is a commitment; when we give our word, we are expected to uphold it. Don't let your word define you as unreliable. As much as possible, keep your word.

God always honors His word and expects the same from us. Making empty promises is never advisable; it's always better to do what needs to be done. Broken promises erode respect and trust.

Consider what would have happened if God had retracted His promise at the cross. Knowing our flaws and imperfections, He could have decided otherwise. However, He upheld His promise, enduring the cross and its associated suffering for our sake.

In the movie "Liar Liar," Jim Carrey portrays Fletcher Reede as a compulsive liar whose inability to lie disrupts his life and relationships. This example highlights how failing to keep one's word can damage relationships and trust.

For example, I had a friend who lied incessantly. Despite my affection for her, her words held no value for me. I strive to be seen as trustworthy and honest; my word is crucial. I've always endeavored to fulfill promises made to my children, unwilling to disappoint them with unkept promises.

Similarly, God keeps His promises to us. As stated in 2 Peter 3:9, *"The Lord is not slow in keeping his promise, as some understand slowness. Instead, he is patient with you, not wanting anyone to perish, but everyone to come to repentance."* God's patience and grace are boundless, offering us many chances for redemption.

Lamentations 3:22-23 (NIV) echo this sentiment: *"Because of the LORD's great love we are not consumed, for his compassions never fail. They are new every morning; great is your faithfulness."*

God's love for us is immense, even when we fall short. He died for us while we were still flawed and sinful. My prayer is to emulate God's truthfulness and integrity, aspiring to be known for honesty and an excellent reputation.

Lord, help me keep my word.

Conclusion

⁓

My fellow Christians, each chapter in this book was crafted with you in mind, reflecting the sentiment of Hebrews 10:25: *"Not forsaking the assembling of ourselves together, as the manner of some is; but exhorting one another: and so much the more, as ye see the day approaching."* My primary goal was to share wisdom about persevering, staying committed, expressing love for God and others, standing firm in faith, and maintaining trust in Christ throughout your journey.

While many Believers may not be transparent, highlighting my trials is the most effective way to share my testimony as a believer. Like weight loss success stories, which are more convincing when accompanied by before-and-after visuals, the success stories in the Bible and those of our forefathers serve as tangible guides on our spiritual path. I am grateful for the sermons and teachings of countless leaders who have laid the groundwork for us for centuries.

In this book, I've spotlighted individuals who steadfastly held onto their faith, showing us we, too, can remain faithful and uphold our commitments even in the face of adversity.

Like Paul, we are ambassadors for Christ, representing Him in all we do. Whatever your calling:

- If you're a writer, write prolifically to spread the good news.
- If you're a missionary, go out and compel men and women to come to Christ.
- If you're a preacher, preach the Gospel in the sanctuary and wherever you are.
- If you're hospitable, extend your kindness without reservation.
- If you're a musician, play, sing, and minister with all your God-given talent.

2 Timothy 4:2 (ESV) instructs, *"Preach the word; be ready in season and out of season; reprove, rebuke, and exhort, with complete patience and teaching."* Seize every opportunity to share with others. Remember, you were created to glorify God and make Him known to all who are lost.

About the Author

Daphanny Denette C. Baker, originally from Plant City, Florida, was raised by the late Rev. Clifford and Mother Alean Porter in Newark, New Jersey. She began singing at six and has been actively involved in church since accepting salvation at fifteen. A 1988 graduate of Ewing High School in Trenton, New Jersey, Daphanny pursued a career in cosmetology and maintained her license to this day. She holds a bachelor's degree in Criminal Justice, applying her knowledge in corrections. She also boasts a Master's in Business Administration (MBA).

Daphanny has directed many foreign and domestic choirs, serving as a state, district, and local minister of music. Known as a "True Worshipper," she is passionate about leading God's people to new heights in their worship experience. In 1999, Daphanny answered her call to ministry and was licensed as an Evangelist Missionary in the Church of God in Christ in 2007.

Lady Baker's love for the Lord is evident in her dedication to helping women in pain. She believes that "scarred hands heal best" and that God has used her past struggles to bring healing to this generation. On May 25th, 2013, she married Bishop Melvin T. Baker, and together they have five incredibly talented children: Yonna, Rey, Diamond, LJ, and Jared. And my one granddaughter, Ani'yah Reyana.

As the Chairlady of women in her local church, Lady Baker is deeply involved in the Women's Ministry, collaborating diligently with her husband. Recently elevated to the Office of Elder, her every endeavor is geared towards building the Kingdom of God at the Temple of Praise Cathedral Church of God in Christ.